TROUBLE
SHOOTER

TROUBLE SHOOTER

60/60

– PEACE KEEPING TECHNIQUES FOR
CONFLICTS IN THE WORKPLACE –

KATHEY BATEY

DEDICATION

*To anyone who has ever found themselves in
conflict and wish they knew a better way out than
tears or fists. Dedicated to peace in your world
in business, relationships, parenting,
marriage and community.*

CONTENTS

"Blessed are the peacemakers;
For they shall be called the
Children of God."

Note from Kathey

Conflict is universal, it happens between countries, between states, in communities, schools, businesses, within homes, and even conflict within self. This booklet is your reference guide to help you see conflict as opportunity to strengthen teams and develop people. Conflict should never be a means to destroy, but a way to build up.

Kathey Batey
Spirited Presentations LLC
www.SpiritedPresentations.com
www.DivorceSupportAnonymous.com
PO Box 150286
Grand Rapids MI 49515
810 730 6679

1
TECHNIQUES-
PREVENTIONS OF CONFLICT

PREVENTION
The best argument is the one that never happens.

1

Is the environment you work in open to being vulnerable? Have they mastered the art form of admitting mistakes? This creates freedom to be authentic and builds connection to form a team. Connection creates cohesiveness, lowering the potential for conflict.

2

Be the peacemaker, the calming voice, the wise source, the encourager. Notice when people do things right. Out loud.

3

Do you laugh enough in your office? Or are you always on task? Do you have mental breaks as a team to lighten the tone and relieve some stress? If you laugh together you have better chances troubleshooting together during conflict.

4

Do you betray confidences when you are trusted with them? Do you note personal shortcomings of others? Do you not include part of the team on team decisions and group outings? These are some of the factors which create an unsafe environment that builds walls of suspicion and is ripe and ready for conflict.

5

Do you create an atmosphere for beautiful apologies? Apologies that flow free and easy within the workplace? Or does pride refrain this social grace?

6

Do you encourage risk and tolerate failure? Striving for excellence is different than unyielding perfectionism. At the end of the day, we're all humans who need to be part of a work community. Unless its brain surgery, financial security or dealing with explosives, allow there to be the grace of the human element.

7

Do you extend grace? Overlook a matter that will not do damage to the company? It will build your company.

Do you fear conflict so you don't say something that will do damage to the company? It will tear down your company.

Being afraid of conflict can create conflict and allow for office bullies.

8

Confirm communication to minimize mis-
communication. It only takes a simple question to make sure you are understood. Ask
for feedback. Don't assume because you
think you stated it clearly everyone gets your
intent.

9

Praise publicly, reprimand privately.

Shame lies delicately beneath the skin.

10

Do you truly respect the individual or is it just part of the third paragraph of your mission statement? How do you demonstrate that respect? Do you respect the differences in individuals? How is this shown in your workplace?

11

Trust is a great way to prevent conflict. Is the leadership trusted? Does the leadership lead, promote and praise people or do they prefer minimal contact? Email does not establish relationships, it filters it.

12

Is this a safe environment? Do you see conflict rising and take the time necessary to
reassure integrity of the leadership, the
policies and the people around you? Do you
overlook integrity and character issues? If
you do, you are making an unstable workplace and it is only a matter of time before
you will have conflict.

13

Have you established the steps for grievance in your company?
Do people believe they will be heard or are they fearing blatant or subtle retribution? Are the steps for grievance the same in action as they are in the employee handbook?

14

Valuing other people, their interests, their skills create an environment better suited for facing conflict. Feelings of being devalued will be amplified in conflict. Give honor to all people.

15

Do you have a close friend at work? Or
do you shut yourself off and stay isolated?
When we don't allow ourselves to be known
we can build suspicions which can lead to
conflict. No man is an island. We need to
part of the team.

16

Do you celebrate successes beyond merely stating "good job!" Celebrating builds strong teams which are better able to handle conflict as a team. It only takes a piece of candy and a voice of excitement to create celebration (and you can even do without the candy).

17

Stay emotionally healthy. Don't allow yourself or others to become cynical, or slight other people at work. Stress will come, conflict will happen. You need to be emotionally healthy to be the most prepared for conflict. Take your breaks, eat your lunch away from the desk. Have times to recreate your energy.

18

Be quick to reach out for help when things go haywire. The longer you keep it secret the bigger it can become and more conflict it can create. Asking for advice or input helps build a team.

19

Is there a blame/shame mentality in your workplace? Are you ready and willing to place blame when things go wrong? This dynamic only adds to the conflict when it arises. Be more interested in a solution than pointing fingers at who is at fault. Practice finding solutions together. This practice will be most helpful when conflicts come.

20

What have you settled for, for too long? A peacemaker guards and protects peace, but does not tolerate injustice or harm.

2
TECHNIQUES-
MANAGING ARISING CONFLICT

There is no story without conflict. Every
conflict has opportunity for discovery of
self, discovery of others and discovery of life.

21

When conflict or the potential of conflict arises, the company structure and boundaries will be tested. Watch closely to find what boundaries need to be strengthened or need to change. Will your policies, procedures and leadership hold back the fire? Or are they vague and so politically correct they provide no guidance?

22

Listen to the emotions of the conflict as much as the words. What do you hear? Fear? Anger? Injustice? Is the person being heard? How do you confirm they are being heard? Use reflective statements, "Jim, what I hear you saying is…" Let them know they are being heard and you want to hear their thoughts and ideas to resolve the conflict. Listening respectfully can stop the issue from escalating further.

23

Open palms- What are your hands doing during the rising of a conflict. Open posture, open palms show an openness of mind.

24

Do you listen? Or are you in a rush to "fix it"? Ask the question, "What happened?" Without judgment listen. Truly listen to people's point of view.

25

Swords are easy to draw in conflict. Swords never fix anything, they just bloody everyone. Your defenses are your sword, keep them down until necessary.

26

Your response, "This is the way it's always been done", is a sure way to set up a company for failure in your employees eyes. It leads to distrust and detachment.

27

Is there something that can be negotiated within the conflict? What is set in stone and what needs to be reconsidered?

28

Stay away from "you should", or "you need to". These words only causes defenses to rise and conflict to heighten.

29

Find small things you can agree on (regard-less how small). Conquer the small ones first to illustrate agreements can be reached and you've opened the lines of communication.

30

Have you agreed on the problem?
Sometimes people disagree with the problem as much as the solution. Spend the
time necessary to identify and articulate the
problem. Clarify the problem and regard
any underlying problem that is creating
workplace chaos.

31

Instead of getting defensive, get curious. Ask questions for clarification. Understand the heart behind the conflict. Questions open dialogue. Statements will often close it off.

32

"We have a problem" not "You have a problem". Give conflict a team mentality. This can be an opportunity to build your team and make it stronger. Conflict = opportunity.

33

"If you are patient in one moment of anger, you will escape a hundred days of sorrow."

Chinese proverb

34

"A gentle answer turns away wrath, but a harsh word stirs up anger."

Proverbs 15:1

35

Gentleness is strength. What will guide you
now is the way you control yourself within
the situational dynamics. Hold your stance
physically gentle, but girded with strength to
stand for what is right. Seek justice humbly.

36

Ask more questions, make fewer statements. "What happened? What can we do to correct it? Can you give me options to be considered?"

37

Don't be afraid of the pause. Let people think, stress shuts down the brain to fight, flight or freeze. Take the necessary time to breathe. Silence is golden and it can be powerful.

38

Respect peoples perspective regardless how foreign it seems to you. They have their own reasons for believing the way they do and we may never know the background of where their anger initiated and why. So respect is always the safest way to resolution of conflict. When anger appears respond with respect.

39

Respect people's personal space. Don't get too close – it shows threat, don't stand too far away, it shows fear.

40

Follow up on the people in conflict when
it is resolved to insure this issue is resolved
and not just stuffed somewhere to explode
later.

3
TECHNIQUES-
DEESCALATING
CONFLICT

When you feel tempted to be defensive, be
inquisitive instead.

41

Bring the individuals into a private space
to hear their story. Ask "what happened?"
Don't ask "why", it can create defensive-
ness. Let the dynamics unfold. Prioritize
the issues. Listen for the solvable elements
of the conflict to work on first together. Do
you have all the information?

42

What is your physical demeanor in conflict?
If you are heightened in responsive anger,
the conflict will get worse. Use a gentle
answer in contrast to the anger or objection
coming at you. If you fight anger with anger
you will only fuel the fire.

43

"Is there any valid point to the counterargument?" Put the person in the opposition's shoes. Sometimes this can help them gain another's perspective when the opposition speaks.

44

Is there a scarcity of resources, freedom or position that is causing the conflict? Identify it, discuss it. Is it real? How can it be given more information or options? If they come up with the problem, let them be involved in the resolution.

45

When conflicts begin to escalate into angry reactions, they often stop being productive. Take a break, a time out. Give everyone some space to gather their thoughts.

46

During escalating conflict, stick to the facts and keep the emotions as minimal as possible. At a later time check on those emotions when people are not swimming in them. Don't ignore them because someone may be drowning from them alone, quietly.

47

A calm response is not your natural reaction, it will require concentrated effort on your part.

"Fools rush in where angels fear to tread." Tread softly.

48

Conflict and anger are not the problem. What we do with conflict can become the problem. Remember conflict = opportunity.

49

Empathize with their feelings and not their behavior. Ask, "Is there a better way to handle this?" Respect whatever you hear. Value their opinion and you can win an ally.

Learn to disagree respectfully where they are.

50

Word choice matters. Select those words which give hope, encouragement and movement toward resolution. Orders and demands only raise defenses and shut down discussion. Help them be in the process to discover better options and avoid passive aggressive behavior later on.

51

Normalize their protest and anger. "I see you are angry about this decision. I understand this is not what you wanted to see happen nor what you worked for."

Don't make them prove themselves, or their emotions, accept them. It can soften the anger.

52

When people feel powerless they will grasp for anything that can give them power. This could be another co-worker or secrets never spoken. Listen to the emotions. We can all become children when conflict escalates. Be the grown up of guidance. See beyond the pain. Listen for doable actions.

53

We must re-engage the frontal brain when anger arises. We can become primal when anger gets out of control and function from our primal (limbic) brain. Give them a minute to pause, breathe and re-engage their logic.

54

Watch your reactions in your face and body.
Are you overreacting? It can ignite even
more vitriol.

55

If authority is challenged, bring the conver-
sation back to the issue. Address the issue
first. When the issue is resolved, define and
discuss the necessity for the order of authority. Work within the boundaries of the
authority.

56

If things become belligerent and disruptive, offer concise, respectable choices. Deflect personal attacks to polices and bylaws which you cannot control.

57

When things get out of control, stick to the facts of the situation to keep it grounded.

58

Be careful your assumptions don't carry you away from the truth. Listen to intuition, but proceed with caution with your assumptions. They may be filled with bias which exacerbates misunderstanding.

59

Give ultimatums carefully, don't insist on anything you can't reinforce. Don't box people in a corner so they have to fight themselves out.

60

Ask yourself, "What will matter 1 year from now?" Relationships will matter. Conflict gives us an opportunity to reevaluate our workplace, our relationships, our values and priorities. Keep what is important-important. You will never regret honoring and listening to people during conflict. Even if the conflict does not resolve.

Keynotes & Trainings

Four Ways to Argue Effectively-
Conflict Communication

Mediation in The Workplace-
For Management & Staff

Having The Time of Our Lives-
Living Out Our Priorities

The 30s, 40s & 50s-
The Decades of our Lives

Other Books and programs by Kathey Batey
For more information visit our website
www.SpiritedPresentations.com or
www.DivorceSupportAnonymous.com

About the Author

Kathey Batey is a Corporate Trainer, Consultant, Facilitator and Domestic Mediator. She has been speaking and training since 2004.

Kathey is the founder of *Divorce Support Anonymous* support groups and webinars for people going through life changes. She inspires leveraging change and a perspective that allows people to find opportunity in life's challenges.

She is the author of 8 books and workbooks and has appeared on television and radio as a featured speaker. She facilitates *Divorce Support Anonymous* groups and *ReDesigning Your Life* workshops that has helped hundreds of men and women through divorce, death of a spouse, empty nest, job loss and other life changes.

Kathey delivers practical messages with inspirational quips, practical ideas, and attitude awareness to use change as leverage to pursue a fulfilled life.